CAREER REIMAGINED: *A practical course for clarity and alignment in your best work lane*

INTRODUCTION...

Finding your ideal vocation is more of a pathway than a destination.

The goal here is to define your path and move in a more aligned direction towards your best life from a holistic approach, focusing on designing a life, not just getting a job.

Through strategic questioning, you will build your own personal profile page specific to your ideal life creation. You will also discover which work style you prefer, gain understanding as to why previous jobs have not been a match, as well as define other personal skills, traits and preferences.

Current statistics reveal around 54% are unhappy in their jobs as of this release; other studies report as high as 87% are not engaged or happy in their work.

You can't squeeze a round peg into a square hole....nor should you continue to try.

Clues someone is the wrong career/job

- Experiencing anything from mild frustration to rage or general bitchiness
- No energy for anything outside of work, withdrawal from social activities etc.
- A general lack of caring about yourself or others (like your heart is shrinking)
- Feeling constantly under stress (whether the job is stressful or not)
- Reoccurring illness/days calling off work/weight gain or other physical symptoms (80% of health problems are stress related)
- Loathing Mondays and living for the weekend
- Constant mental battle, feeling indecisive, often vacillating back and forth, or a sense of self-betrayal
- Say things like "it's just a job" or "there are worse jobs out there"
- In autopilot, unconscious or asleep in your life
- Likely to take up bad habits or addictions to manage stress or boredom
- Feeling like a slave, prisoner or martyr (general victimhood)
- Tendency to blame others for unhappiness, bad boss, economy, lack of education etc.

If you identify with some of these above- I feel you, I have been there- I was living with most of these symptoms myself at one time or another.

Evidence of the right career lane

- The feeling of peace is evident, like you are in the right lane! (this is huge)
- Your quality of life improves dramatically!
- Improved health and reduced stress!
- You stop fighting yourself!
- You look better and feel better!
- Life flows more easily!
- You have more energy!
- Your heart is expansive, increasing your capacity to love those around you!
- Increased sense of contribution and fulfillment!
- You feel like you matter when what you do matters!
- You like every day, instead of living for only 1-2 days out of 7!
- You are a better version of yourself!
- You use your strengths instead of glaring at your weaknesses!
- You have more passion!
- You have more of a sense of freedom!
- Other areas of your life improve and you attract more good into your life!
- You will feel more alive and present!
- You live more consciously, from your heart!
- You feel at ease and enjoy greater health and wellbeing!
- Bad habits lessen without even noticing!
- You are excited to get up in the morning and get to your work!

WHAT YOU WILL NEED:

A journal or paper for taking notes (or computer). You will be asked a question and devise your answer in a notebook, journal or laptop etc. This won't take up too much space- a few pages in an A4 notebook or Word doc should suffice.

Also set aside one or two pages- either at the front or the back of your notebook- somewhere easy to get to, as this will be your "Hotlist" which will become your personal profile page.

You can break the course up how you choose, either contemplate one idea per day or go through the course in one or two sittings if you prefer. The more thought you put into each question, the better your end result will be.

Don't rush

Dig deep

Let's get started...

2 requests while going through Section 1...

1) Forget about "making money" while doing this section (you can still have money based answers as appropriate) but don't try to figure out the money making part- just yet.
2) Forget about the "what" or the "how" for now.
   And just play...

Explore all the possibilities and see what comes up.

Clarity first. Clarity is really important, we need to know clearly what we want so we don't wander about aimlessly.

Get clear about what lights you up.

SECTION ONE

1) WHAT DO YOU LOVE?

Let's start with an easy one...

This is a total random, brainstorming of activities, interests, tasks, and subjects that you like, love, or enjoy doing.

List anything and everything you can think of.

Here are some ideas to get you started: interests, hobbies, outdoors, sciences, learning, technology, spirituality, arts, places, and things.

Make a list in your notebook.

Now take your **favorite** and add it to your **Hotlist** page that you have set aside. (Or 2 or 3 if you can't decide on only 1)

*Name each topic (and number if you like) on your hotlist, so that when you look back at it you will know what each answer corresponds to.

2) WHAT ARE YOU GOOD AT?

List anything and everything you at good at...
Your strengths, anything you find easy, pick-up quickly- be random, be exhaustive from the smallest thing to the most obvious.
Include your strengths in your current/ most recent job...
What have people commented on before?
Have you won awards?
Ideas: fixing, designing, problem solving, selling, networking...
(Forget about whether it fits into "work" or looks like a job- stay in creative land).

EXAMPLE: online marketing, Interior design, organizing, encouraging others, etc.

Write a list in your notebook.

When you are done with your list- look back at it and consider- what are you BEST at?
What do you do better than anything else? Is it on your list already?
Maybe you can ask a couple of close people you trust what they think you do best.

BEST AT: problem solving technical issues.
Add the one thing you believe you are BEST at to your **Hotlist.** (Keep it more general if hard to define right now, for example "communication" if most of your answers revolve around writing, journalism, blogging etc.).

Feel free to add any new ideas to your list that come to you during the day.

3) THE MATCHING GAME

Here we play the matching game.
Match what you love and what you are good/best at together.
This is your wheelhouse, or a major indicator of where you need to be- the intersection of skill and passion.
Take question 1 and 2 and play the matching game, pairing anything that appears on both lists and create a new shortlist here of those (this might be redundant from the last question- but check anyway)
Make sure you both like it and are good at it- you want both.
Take 1 or 2 top matches and add them to your **Hotlist** page.
Call it something like: 3) love and skills combo, so you know what this is referring to when you look back at the completed list. (You are creating your profile page).

4) CAREER MUSINGS

What did you want to be when you grew up?
Do you remember being asked that question?
The one that adults love to ask kids…
Recall anything you considered being possible options at some point from very young, up to present day- anything you can remember counts.
From 2 to 20 –either is good; the more you can recall the better.
Think back to early memories about this and work your way forward. (The order doesn't matter)
What could you see yourself doing, or becoming?

A) Make your list down the page like this (example) in your notes

EXAMPLE:

ER Doctor

Circus Performer

Hairstylist

Etc.

Do this now...

  B) Once your list is complete down the page, next to each job/career put a word or sentence that describes what *appealed* to you about each idea, anything that attracted you to this type of work (past or present).

The **"why" EXAMPLE**: ER Doctor= helping people, the title/prestige, excitement, physical activity, money.

C) Now, look at the completed list of your whys...

> What words, feelings or ideas repeat themselves?
> Put the most repeated words into a short list.
> For example did you keep mentioning physical jobs or helping people? Which "why" repeated?
> Now add your top 3 favorite reasons to your **Hotlist**.

5) **CHILDHOOD ACTIVITIES**

  A) What did you like to do when you were a child?
  List all the activities you were involved in, or if you weren't very involved- what would you have liked to do...

  Do that now in your notebook.

  B) Once you have your exhaustive list, drill down to similar repeat type of activities- what were your main/common themes?

EXAMPLE: movement, competition, productivity, connection, excitement, variety. (Or you can keep it simple: art, music, sport- general answers).

Add 1-3 most common themes to your **Hotlist**.

6) NO-FLY ZONE

Also important to clarify – what **don't** you like to do professionally or what types of environments do you know to avoid?

(This may be easier if you have tried a few things and found they weren't for you, slightly more challenging for anyone with less experience). Do the best you can.

Most of us can tell without even doing it what would or would not appeal to us (i.e. tightrope walking or coal mining).

What is your bottom line, what won't you do? It's good to get clear about this too!

- A) Make a list of things you really don't like doing or environments you know you wouldn't thrive in, anything that is a big fat No for you.

EXAMPLE: Highly stressful environments, small confined spaces, graveyard shift etc.

Do that now in your notebook.

B) Then once you have your list…
Look for themes, general feelings to avoid and make a smaller list of things you prefer/need in the positive. (Because we are building your profile, it is focused on the positive).

EXAMPLE: I prefer a flexible schedule; I need a supportive team; I like to work independently etc.
Add your most important items to your **Hotlist.**

7) CONTRIBUTION

How do you like to contribute or serve others?

One of the basic human needs is "contribution." This is why (generally speaking) most of us feel better when we work or have something to do, particularly when it is something we enjoy, that feeling of satisfaction, a sense of accomplishment or contribution.

There are 1000 ways to contribute or serve or help, so how do you prefer to do that do you think? Where do you shine when it comes to helping others? What are your unique gifts when it comes to other people? What form does it typically take? (This should be a mutually gratifying experience). Anything you have ever done to help, or thought of doing in the future counts.

EXAMPLE: Fix bicycles, help elderly neighbors, text sick friends, encouraging others, cooking for others, gift giving, etc.

Do this now in your notebook.

Once you have your short list, add your favorite to your **Hotlist.**

8) WHO ARE YOUR PEOPLE?

Who are the people or sub-group of people that you feel a connection to? Is there a particular demographic of people you feel like you "get them" or have a way with them? This can be a professional niche or co-workers (not necessarily those less fortunate).

It can be any sub-group from newborns to the elderly, homeless or highly successful people and anyone in between. You can expand this list to include animals or even plants if you like, since they are living too.

Ideas: babies, toddlers, gifted children, sporty teens, college age, young professionals, working adults, women, men, single parents, working families, business people, entrepreneurs, middle age, minorities, gay/lesbian/transgender, another ethnic group, homeless, newly divorced, addicts, autistic/special needs, hospice, elderly. (I think it is okay to include animals here too- maybe you are drawn to help or work with horses, cats or snakes)?

Add your shortlist or the one particular group that stands out, to your **Hotlist**.

PEOPLE vs. TASK

Are you more "People Orientated or "Task Orientated?"

If you had to break your work day into 2 percentages out of 100, what percentage of your work day do you think you would like to spend around other people, interacting or working with directly in some way? From 0-100%... what is your ideal amount of time based on an 8 hour day?

What percentage would you prefer to be working on a focused task, based on the same work day? From 0-100%.

This should add up to 100% so something like 80-20, 60-40, or 50-50.

This answer can change over time (younger people often prefer more people interaction) depending on the intensity of the particular job/demands from other people etc.

There is no right or wrong here, just consider your preference. You can also have some days where you might really crave time with people and other days where you prefer to be alone, so you may prefer to come up with some kind of sliding scale. Typically, outgoing people like to be around people more and introverted people prefer to be busy with a task rather than being pulled on/interacting with others as much.

Now add your percentage to your **Hotlist** page (noting which is higher, task or people)

9) WHO WOULD YOU LIKE TO BECOME?

Close your eyes and imagine yourself 3-5 years from now in your best role and life…

What does it look like? Where are you? What are you doing?

Picture this image often and sit in the feeling of it, (even if you feel a long way off from this).

What traits do you possess in this picture of you living your best life? Are you calmer and more confident perhaps? The more you look at this image of yourself the more you will gravitate towards it naturally. (It's best to look at images of what we want, not what we are trying to avoid). Move into that calm confident energy- wear the clothes now, embody *that* person now- you don't have to wait.

Write a short description of how you will feel (but in the present tense) and add this to your **Hotlist**. "I am…"

10) HOW DO YOU LIKE TO WORK?

We all thrive in different environments; pick your preference from this list.

- Working quietly, autonomously where you do everything yourself
- In a group, as a member of a team
- In a partnership, as equals
- Second in charge, supporting the visionary
- The leader/owner/boss, or manager where others report to you

Add your answer to your **Hotlist**. (You may have a different answer to the list provided)

11) LEFT vs. RIGHT

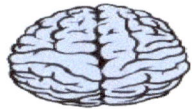

Left side of the brain vs right side of the brain- which side do you prefer to work from? Perhaps you are a combo, if so which one is more often leading than the other?

Left side: head, thinker, analytical, critical, judging, numbers, organized, scheduled, facts, order.

Right side: emotion, pictures, imagination, creativity, feeling, sensing, free, expansive, flowing, head in the clouds.

EXAMPLE: mainly left side, with right side activities sort out as hobbies.

Add your findings to your **Hotlist.**

12) WHERE DO YOU PREFER TO LIVE?

There are many options in ways and places to live, without getting too specific...

But let's cover the basics

City, suburbs, beach, small town, country, off-grid, traveling full time, tiny home, or a motorhome.

Pick your favorite place to live, with a secondary if you like or can't decide between the two.

Add your preference to your **Hotlist.**

13) YOUR IDEAL DAY

A) What would you do with MOST of your time if you had enough money to never HAVE to work again?

Many people instantly say "travel," to this question. Which tends to come from the souls need to expand and can be the most obvious choice especially if currently confined in your job. If you would say travel as well as a first response, then consider what you might do once you are done with say- a year on the road. Then what would the perfect day look like to you? What are all the wonderful things you would do in your ideal day?

Write it out in list form down the page like this...

EXAMPLE:

Take coffee back to bed and get up slowly

Go for a walk in nature

Take a bath

Ride a motorcycle

Go shopping

Write a chapter for your biography

Etc.

Now write your day out like this in your notebook

- B) Once you have your list. Now next to each activity, add the feelings or motivation that goes along with it

EXAMPLE:

Take coffee back to bed= comforting, ease into the day

Go for a walk in nature= relaxing, energizing, recharge, mental clarity

The second part of the list is just as important- because it is the feeling we get from something that is the motivation to do the activity itself. Do you see a pattern emerging? Are there key words that keep coming up?

Do you include both tension and release activities? We need both on a daily basis or we tend to get bored- something to think about.

Add the top 3 reoccurring themes to your **Hotlist**.

14) Daily Practice- non negotiables

This may have come up in the last question…but needs its own attention.

What are your daily practices to maintain a sense of wellbeing and balance? Activities that need to be in your life, your non-negotiables?

What do you feel really good if you do vs. not right if you don't? Make time, give it room in your life (these are not usually work related), but important practices or 3, that you need in your daily life.

Ideas: taking your time in the mornings, alone time, walking, meditation, quiet time, journaling, affirmations, creative visualization, breathing exercises, prayer, reading, gratitude, exercise, yoga etc.

Add to your **Hotlist**.

16) WORK PERSONALITY TYPES

Here are 6 key work styles created to describe different aptitudes. 1 or 2 will stand out to you, most people are a combination.

Have a read through these 6 and decide which are your strongest matches, which do you identify with the most?

PRACTICAL

- Likes to work with tools, motors, building supplies or machines of any kind. Typically not as highly social or people orientated in their work, more on the task orientated side; likes to be productive and see results.

- Good skills/natural ability working with mechanical, electrical, machinery, problem solving, repair work, building, engineering, farming, or cooking. Usually works with equipment they can touch and see, these people like to work with their hands and are pragmatic, usually down-to-earth, practical types.
- Needs: time and space to focus, to feel productive and see concrete results.
- Consider: not everyone has to be as productive; it's okay to just BE and not always have to DO; rest and consider creative pursuits for fun, as they will serve this type well.

TRADITIONAL

- Likes structure, is happy working in an office or structured environment usually with numbers, documents, charts and graphs, in a set orderly way; appreciates rules and regulations and prefers things done right. These people are typically in accounting, Information Technology based jobs, human resources, office management, law, administration, retail, or warehouse workers.
- Generally avoids ambiguous, unstructured jobs and prefers to work for a business/other people and sees it as the "safe choice".
- Is good at "task orientated" work in formal settings, often perfectionist types that like systems and order, who prefer to compartmentalize their lives.
- Needs: the stability of a steady income and potential career advancement of working for someone else; prefers to follow a set plan and sees life in a more conservative, traditional manner, likes predictability.
- Consider: thinking outside the box; pursuing creative endeavors outside of work; relax/take vacations and not only work all the time.

SCIENTIST

- Loves to be constantly learning, studying, researching, digging deep and finding answers particularly math or science related, physics or any myriad of other science subjects.

- Is good at understanding and solving problems, values proven facts more so than other theories like spirituality or more ethereal concepts. Identifies self as intellectual, precise, studious and scientific; likes facts, general knowledge and trivia. Prefers more task orientated work rather than intensive people interaction, can also work as a professor driven more by the information itself and sharing of ideas.

- Needs: facts and hard evidence, to be right, likes to prove a point with scientific backing, to be seen as an intellectual and always continues to learn.

- Consider: Others beliefs and points of view and not see others as below them; it's okay to leave room for faith or emotion. This type needs to not take everything too seriously and remember to laugh.

CREATIVE

- Likes creative activities in the arts, often involved in one or many of the following: creative writing, painting, online web/design, poetry, music/musical instruments, sound mixing, producing, dance, acting/drama, hairdressing, or crafts. Prefers freedom and variety, avoids rigidity or mundane repetitive routine.

- Sees value in artistic communication, resists dry, uninspired communication wherever possible; feels the need to express themselves in their own unique creative way.

- Needs: independence, freedom, self-expression and creative outlets.

- Consider: not becoming too ethereal/impractical, maintain some organization particularly with home/ time/ finances, and respect less creative people.

HELPER

- Likes helping or serving others: caregiving, teaching, nursing, healer, doctor, holistic worker, customer service, yoga instructor, counseling, training, or providing information. Generally avoids heavy task orientation, prefers to work with people for their betterment and enjoys the personal reward of such work.

- Is good at taking care of people, teaching/training or helping in any way, and takes a genuine interest, values people and solving social problems, often gets involved in social issues and reform.

- Needs: contribution, purpose, connection, to help and see others benefiting etc.

- Consider: can be too much of a "fixer" and become depleted, needs to not overcommit or feel overly responsible for others and take time for themselves.

ENTREPRENEUR

- Driven to lead and succeed, prefers the freedom of self-employment or partnerships. Usually a natural salesperson- persuasive or inspiring. Thinks/sees the big picture with ease and typically doesn't like being bogged down in the details or the fine print.
- Is good at leading and inspiring others, selling products, ideas or services.
- Values success in business, leadership, politics or sport; is energetic, ambitious, and capable.
- Needs: to feel successful and productive, likes to develop their own brand/product/services and to build something, doesn't like to feel tied down to other peoples schedules or work for others.
- Consider: resting more; not being too aggressive or controlling, delegating the detailed work; and not judging people who are not as driven as them.

Which stood out to you? Figure out your 1st, 2nd and 3rd - In order of what feels most like you, or if you have 1 or 2 equally important ones, that's typical. Then add them to your **Hotlist**. (Most of us will be a blend of 2, or a predominant type- this can change also depending on age and stage etc.)

17) YOUR TIME LINE

Using your life as a guide... when we look back we can often see breadcrumbs that led us to where we are now.

Make a list of major life events that you can remember, starting from birth up to present day. Include child events, memorable jobs/job changes, moves, guideposts, turning points- lifestyle chances etc. Add anything that comes to you whether seemingly significant or not. It doesn't have to be perfect or even chronologically accurate, just do your best.

EXAMPLE:

1975: Born

1978: Moved to Nebraska

1981: Played baseball loved it, played the rest of my life...

1986: Parents divorced, moved in with my aunt for 1 year

1992: Coached my brothers soccer team

Once you have completed the timeline, look at it and see if you can see any clues, any people or tasks that kept coming to you or anything that connects the dots for you now. (This may come to you later). None of your life so far need be wasted; it has all culminated to make you who you are today giving you the exact experience and skills that you need for your next adventure.

You can add anything that was a major marker or any Ah-ha's to your **Hotlist** (optional).

15) PAIN INTO PURPOSE (last question)

This may be a tricky question, but important as I will explain. (A personal question for a very good reason).

What was your most traumatic childhood event or wound?

Identify what you think it was, in a word or a sentence?

We typically spend years trying to heal it whether consciously or sub-consciously, and then either sooner or later will help others come out of similar pain. There are a 1000 ways that can be outworked and not necessarily as a career, but helpful to recognize. This is likely to be a subconscious driver in determining how you fit.

Put it into a dialogue like this…

EXAMPLE: I felt neglected

Then turn it into a positive. "I would like to help people be seen, heard and feel like they matter."

Add your statement of intent to your **Hotlist.**

Great job, you are now mostly done with creating your profile page- (feel free to add more if you like)

SECTION 2...BRINGING IT ALL TOGETHER

THE JUICE

Look at your hotlist – this is your now your personal profile page, pointers to a more meaningful life.

Use your hotlist as a guide or a checklist when considering anything new- (new ideas can spring from this as well).

Go with the 80/20 rule, where you match around 80% in your next venture.

Much less than 80% and you are less aligned and will feel mismatched fairly quickly.

There is usually around 20% of a job that you don't particularly love or aren't your strongest skillset. Delegate or outsource these tasks if possible or minimize them as best you can, staying closest to your strengths. Focus on the 80% that works and is a match.

Hopefully now you have much more clarity about what you need, how you like to show up in the world, how you like to contribute and to whom etc.

Where you add value, value gets added back to you in monetary form.

CURRENT JOB/CAREER (or your last job)

Since this is a one-size-fits-all course, I have put together a few questions and strategies, so see which resonates with you at this time...

Consider your current role, how well matched are you now that you have more clarity?

Do you believe in what you do, the company, the culture etc.?

Is it a mutually beneficial experience and trading of time for money?

Are you adding value?

What do you *like* about it if you could just keep the good parts?

What would need to change to make your job work for you?
Always be networking and building relationships, it's a good idea, (no matter what is next).
If you don't have a profile on LinkedIn already- I suggest creating one and then connecting with people in your current company.
What can you leverage in your current role to create more of a life you want?
Can you use your current salary to save and fund your own business, study in the meantime and become a Subject Matter Expert in your niche?
It's not always about throwing in the towel completely. Maintain and build your current network, make sure to save your contact list if you can.
Do you need to create an exit strategy with a timeline and financial plan?
Can you become self-employed in the same or related field, or work for another company more in-line with your core values?
Often, people give all their energy to their full time jobs so they don't save any time for things they actually love to do and wind up feeling empty and purposeless.
Maybe adding one night a week to a passionate pursuit would change your whole outlook? Add some side projects or self-study after hours if you can't make a change in the short-term?
Or volunteering Saturday mornings?
Do you already have an idea you have been sitting on that you could begin, even part-time?
If you dream of writing for example- can you start- just 10 minutes a day, writing a blog or private journal?
Is there anything that needs time and attention **before** making a shift?
Maybe you need to clear some mental blocks or do some training before you make any leap?
Some dreams take time and a savings account, so be as organized and well prepared as is necessary for your peace of mind. Jumping ship can backfire if you don't have the guts or the means or both to take the risk right now. So give yourself all the tools and time you need so you have every opportunity to succeed.

ASSEST INVENTORY (Optional)
List your experience in years or months include knowledge, training, skills or experience.
This is good to see, even if it's a short list and all your skills are in one niche- that's okay.
Helpful to look at and see all that you bring to the table. You can use your resume if you like or do this and make sure your resume includes all that you bring to the table (if a general resume is helpful). In most job applications you are better to focus your resume towards a particular job/ vertical (the one you are applying for) this is your sales tool.

NOT WORKING CURRENTLY

If earning money is your primary concern right now, then find the best matching job you can to take care of immediate needs.

If money is not an immediate concern, then you have time to "test the waters" or volunteer or study in your field of choice.

Can you become an expert in a subject? Create a brand around yourself in a particular niche, study everything you can on the subject and then charge low fees initially to get experience consulting, training or teaching others, then gather reviews and market/sell your services/knowledge etc. Or sell products, become a broker/middle seller in a specific market? This can all be done online and there are plenty of courses available that teach specifically step by step.

If you would like resume or interview advice refer to the end of the course.

List of resources: training and freelance/flexible work opportunities

- Free training/scholarships offered by this non-profit, to enhance digital skills for online work- www.samaschool.org
- Freelance design, creative, or editing work @ www.fiverr.com or www.upwork.com
- Freelance practical jobs locally running errands, organizing etc. @ www.taskrabbit.com
- Make and sell crafts, t-shirts, jewelry or any homemade items/products on www.etsy.com
- Drive for Lyft or Uber (requires a car newer than a 2000, ideally with good gas mileage to make it worth it) www.uber.com or www.lyft.com
- Rent out a room in your house through www.airbnb.com (can make up to $100 per night per room)
- Get free stuff (craigslist has a free section) or buy cheaply/renovate/resell on www.Craigslist.org

HOBBY VS CAREER

Look at your hotlist and decide, what is your main theme?
What would you like to do with MOST of your time?
What is also important to you, but will probably be more of a hobby/part time interest/endeavor?

Perhaps you have a hobby that you want to try to take fulltime?

Imagine HAVING to do it every day, does that take the fun out of it for you or are you that passionate about it to want to go full time?

Can you use your next vacation to test the concept and try it full time for a week or two- truly test it out?

Figure out the difference between a hobby and a real career. Sometimes it just wants more time in your life and other times it is a calling. This can be less obvious particularly if you are unhappy in your job and your hobby lights you up. I would still suggest testing it out or adding it into your week instead of waiting until you have more time to do it. If it is that important you will find a way to weave it in. Figure out the difference before you (for example) quit college to become a fulltime poker player. Would the stress outweigh the fun- (especially if you HAD to win to make the rent, versus playing for fun with money from a consistent paycheck)?

Add any helpful conclusions about this idea to your **hotlist** if you want (optional) or you can do color highlighting i.e. orange over full time and green over part time or other important interests or activities like your non-negotiable daily practices for example.

PASSION vs. MONEY

Many people are money driven- gathering wealth and possessions is most important to them, particularly if they are just starting out. Money is a great tool and obviously very necessary.

Ideally we all want and need both- it's possible, plenty of people have it.

I would advise going after your passion FIRST, because this is where your talent and enthusiasm will come together, opening up your creative and natural abilities. *That way adjustments and improvements can be made along the way to build income.* If you are *only* in anything for the money, the passion can leave very quickly and with it any motivation to continue.

If the money is high but the passion is low, we can find it hard to leave, but may feel unfulfilled or out of alignment. In the meantime, fund your passion plan, or save where you are regardless; use your current situation to plan your next venture.

If both are low, it's a no- brainer- do something else! Consider volunteering or breaking into a new industry at the bottom just to get experience you can leverage, or try it out first before making a leap.

If you have an idea and are super passionate about it, make sure there is a market for it first (and you aren't trying to swim in the same pool as giant fish you can't compete with). Before throwing everything you have into it and finding out the hard way. ***The key to success is solving a problem, quieting a fear or meeting a desire...for your employer/customer/client/audience.***

WHAT DID YOU LEARN ABOUT YOURSELF?

I am confident that you had a few ah-ha's along the way by now, and that you have gained greater clarity about your life, work style and preferences? It makes sense that we thrive in certain environments and disengage in others given self- realized information.

If you would like to put it into a paragraph about what you learned you can if you like, just so you are able to clearly articulate it for yourself.

If you want to add it to your **hotlist** in a concise paragraph you can (optional).

GET ROLLING

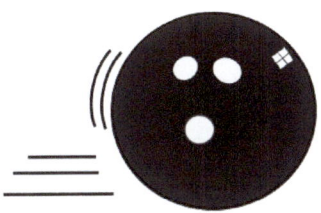

- If you are in a transition period, you may benefit greatly from journaling. Emptying out an over active mind during a time of uncertainty is helpful. Greater clarity and new ideas can also come through journaling.
- Life is a moving target, we are constantly evolving and changing and growing, and that is what is wonderful about this journey and challenging at the same time.
- Even if you are undecided about your exact plan, can you take a small step? Life is like a staircase, you take a step and then you will know what the next is and so on- you don't always know what is at the top of the staircase.
- When you have an idea, move on it- investigate.

- Try to avoid feeling desperate. The world is full of money, opportunities and ways to serve. Desperate feelings or thoughts are going to keep pushing ideas and income away, so stay in a place of gratitude and abundance thinking. There is plenty. You belong here and a way will be made for you.
- What baby step can you take this week to start? If you have started, what can you do next?
- Every week have a plan with 1 or 2 action steps and then hold yourself accountable.
- Do you have an idea? Can you see a need and meet it somehow? Can you answer a fear or meet a desire that people have? What are you knowledgeable about?
- Even if there are other people already doing what you want to do, zig where they zag- it probably won't be exactly the same.
- Surround yourself with people that are where you want to be, look for meetups or join a mastermind group or even challenge yourself with a Toastmasters group to gain confidence and meet likeminded people. We all need support as we navigate forward.
- You are welcome to follow my Facebook page: "On Purpose Career Support," I post daily thoughts to encourage people in this area.
- Do you need more training in your field? There are 1000 ways to gain more knowledge now with the internet- it's all there. Plus an incredible market place for every niche imaginable and whole communities to support you.
- Remember most careers are a path that twists and turns, not an immediate destination, you don't need to have it all figured out.
- You can either start with one little key idea or step, and follow the breadcrumbs as you discover how it unfolds along the way. We don't always get the whole picture. We sometimes have pieces that form as we go. Everyone is different, so just be open and start somewhere.
- But START MOVING, and keep moving.
- Action creates more action which turns into momentum.
- Are you willing to take less money to break into a new industry, leveraging your current skillset?
- Use social media to put the word out there, let people know what you are wanting to do or what field interests you.
- Is there someone you respect in your field of interest, you can take to lunch and pick their brain?
- Do you need some help with interviewing skills or your resume? There are loads of free resources online, just Google your question.
- Don't assume you need a degree, unless you are trying to get into certain credentialed fields, many jobs now prefer experience over a degree. Plenty of highly successful people do not have college educations and avoid hefty student loan debt weighing them down.
- Watch free videos on www.youtube.com whole books are on there about certain subjects, like this famous book I recommend: Think and grow rich by Napoleon Hill. A great book about having the right mindset to create anything you want.

DEALING WITH INSECURITY OR CONFUSION

- There may well be times of frustration or confusion even after doing this course, and I did want to mention that often times your calling might find you as it morphs into shape. This means as you move forward starting at point A, you could gravitate to the left and wind up at point D somewhere completely different doing something unimagined that fits just right. This course may have bought up other options that you are now considering that you hadn't before.
- We go through times of seeming darkness where we literally feel like we can't see anything. If you are in that place right now, hang in there the light will shine again. It may be what I call cocoon time, development time or just timing itself. Don't waste a short season of rest with stressing out, if you are recovering from a stressful period or getting over an illness. Take time, relax your mind and have faith in life supporting you in the process.
- If you are unsure, that is completely normal- sometimes things can just feel wrong for you and that is important to be aware of and not go down certain paths if they feel "off" to you. If you do, you can always turn around again. But you won't *always* know until you try something.
- It is important to have support during times of transition or confusion, take stock and do the best you can to make the best choices and decisions based on your most important needs at the time.
- If you know that for you doing nothing is a recipe for disaster at least keep moving forward. The rest sorts itself out along the way as you go.
- Talk to yourself during insecure times and try to comfort myself with the fact that you have probably been there before and always made it through and you will this time too!
- We are all doing the best we can. Sometimes it is patience that we need, other times it is trying something new, or challenging ourselves. It's up to us to know what we need and what season we are in. It could be any of these: time to train or self-study, rest, retire, regroup, take a leap, change environments or cities, sell a home, or just drop an old limiting belief? Only we can know what is best. We have an inner guide that is very wise, it might just take a little stillness or soul searching to find out. Then follow what feels peaceful and right in your gut.

INSPIRATION & INTUITION

- The "how" is actually the easy part- now you have more clarity, all you need is a little inspiration and that is already in you, it is just a matter of catching it consciously. Now you have cleared the channel for inspiration to flow.
- Inspiration means being "in-Spirit" and that is who you already are anyway. There are many active ways to engage this side of you: being in nature, meditation, doing something creative, yoga, visualization techniques, etc.
- Many people have their most inspired ideas in the shower or driving, because they have created moments of white space- room for inspiration to hit!
- You can simply create some white space by sitting quietly and marinating in all that you love to do. Or get in the shower.
- Once you have your inspiration, take some form of action and/or form a plan, test it out if you can- before making any life altering decisions and use wisdom.
- Remember there are no real failures in life, only a quiet desperate life of undiscovered magnificence!
- Get excited about all the possibilities and don't allow yourself to get down if you feel stuck in something right now. It won't last forever.
- Some may need time to heal after a tough job, breakup or life change, give yourself that time if you need it and nurture yourself- that might be best for you right now.
- Stay open to receiving ideas- it might just be a seed at first. Or you may notice a need in the market that you have never noticed before.
- Every day- ask life, what do you want me to do today?
- Be open to new ideas. Start to prime the pump of ideas, get your creative flow going.
- Every day try to come up with 3 new ideas. They can be about anything – how to improve something, a new product, a new book idea, putting your skills out there to help someone else, anything you can come up with...don't judge it- write it down.
- Keep some ideas to yourself, especially in fledgling stage.

Magic will start happening...
- Encourage yourself, become your loudest cheerleader- yes, talk to yourself out loud!
- You are a Master Creator- capable of amazing and incredible things!
- Life loves enthusiastic people and seems to knock on their door first.

- Keep moving forward, even with multiple ideas and see what keeps lighting up, other ideas may drop away and one or two may stick, follow your instinct.
- Follow what feels good and drop what doesn't as much as you can.
- There will be adjustments along the way, tweak it as you go or realize something isn't right for you. Better to have tried than to have never even attempted.
- Do what makes you happy, and then keep doing more of that…

Thank you for taking the time to get to know yourself better, the world needs what you have to offer…

RESUME AND INTERVIEW ADVICE

Resume tips
- Think of your resume like a sales tool. This is the first of you hiring eyes will see and typically you are up against many other pieces of paper, so make yours count.
- You can "Google" a resume sample template, type over it with your specific experience and save it for your own use.
- Use a "relevant summary" section top and center the can easy be read right away, matching you to the job you are applying for. Make is plain why you are a perfect fit. Use facts and figures, always mention achievements in each role, or have an achievements section near the top, especially if you are in sales or sales based roles.
- If you are attractive, include a small picture in the top right corner, yes it helps- if you have a face for radio- don't include one.

Interview tips
- Arrive early but don't enter the meeting place early as most managers are expecting you on time, definitely don't be late.
- Prior to interviewing, check out the company on Glassdoor.com to make sure it's a positive culture, remember that people often leave reviews if they had negative experiences, but make sure you are not going into a toxic environment *before* you interview. Also it can give you things to check out while you are there or questions to ask about management styles or culture etc.
- Ask about dress code prior to the interview and then wear slightly more formal than the daily normal. Dress codes for interviews vary depending on industry. Err on the side of more dressed up than too casual as this will show you are putting your best image forward. Minimize accessories and makeup- less is more.

- Mirror the energy of the interviewer, if they are calm be calm, if they have more energy then pick it up a little.
- Watch your body language, its super important during interviews. We constantly pick up non-verbal body language. Avoid crossing arms or legs as it can make you look closed off. Maintain good eye contact. Be friendly, and "normal" they are judging you as to if they could work with you every day all day.
- The biggest complaint I hear from interviewers is when candidates reply with overly long rambling answers to questions. Be sure to **listen** to the question being asked and only answer the question. If you answer briefly that is safer and then you can check by saying "Does that answer your question?" Giving the interviewer the opportunity to ask another question or get more info if they need.
- Research the company you are interviewing with, have 2 or 3 good points ready to show you did your homework and are particularly interested in this company and culture etc.
- Know *why* you would be an asset to them and be ready to tell them why.
- Show interest but don't come across as desperate.
- End the interview with the question: "Are there any reservations about hiring me?" That way you have a chance to put them at ease and not leave them wondering if they have a concern.
- Have prepared answers for what is your greatest success or failure, as these are common interview questions. As well as what are your weaknesses, then pick ones that are also positives- like being detail orientated or a perfectionist or work too much something that is partially true but also not a glaring red flag, like living on Facebook all day!
- If you know anyone in the company and you are confident they will put in a good word for you, definitely mention their name (this lowers the risk for the hiring company/manager and can greatly sway their decision in your favor).
- Never talk badly about a previous company or boss, no matter what.

www.ingramcontent.com/pod-product-compliance
Lightning Source LLC
LaVergne TN
LVHW071033070426
835507LV00003B/137